PRAYERS FOR A CHILD'S DAY

compiled by
LAURA RING
illustrated by
JOY ALLEN

© 1999 by Standard Publishing, Cincinnati, Ohio. A division of Standex International Corporation.
Printed in the United States of America. All rights reserved.
Cover design by Matt Key.

06 05 04 03 02 01   5 4 3 2

Library of Congress Catalog Card Number 98-61295
ISBN 0-7847-0891-6
The publishers acknowledge with thanks permission from the following: HarperCollins Publishers for "Dear Father" by
Margaret Wise Brown. © 1943, 1950 by Margaret Wise Brown, renewal © 1978 by Roberta B. Rauch.
Thomas Nelson Publishers for "Lord of the loving heart," first published in 1933 by the Church Missionary Society.
Scriptures marked ICB quoted from the *International Children's Bible, New Century Version,*
© 1986, 1988 by Word Publishing, Dallas, Texas 75039. Used by permission.

Standard
PUBLISHING
CINCINNATI, OHIO

THANK you,
God in heaven,
For a day begun.
Thank you for the breezes,
Thank you for the sun.
For this time of gladness,
For our work and play,
Thank you,
God in heaven,
For another day.

ALL for thee, dear God,
Everything I do,
Or think, or say,
The whole day long,
Help me to be good.

OUR Father which art in heaven,
Hallowed be thy name.
Thy kingdom come.
Thy will be done in earth, as it is in heaven.

Give us this day our daily bread.
And forgive us our debts, as we forgive our debtors.
And lead us not into temptation, but deliver us from evil:
For thine is the kingdom, and the power, and the glory,
For ever. Amen.

DAY by day, dear Lord, of Thee
Three things I pray:
To see Thee more clearly,
To love Thee more dearly,
To follow Thee more nearly,
Day by day.

St. Richard of Chichester

D<small>EAR</small> Father, hear and bless
Thy beasts and singing birds,
And guard with tenderness
Small things that have no words.

Margaret Wise Brown

Lord, teach me all that I should know;
In grace and wisdom I may grow;
The more I learn to do Thy will,
The better may I love Thee still.

Isaac Watts

you made me and formed me with your hands.
Give me understanding so I can learn your commands.

Psalm 119:73, ICB

LORD, help me control my tongue.
Help me be careful about what I say.
Don't let me want to do evil
or join others in doing wrong.

Psalm 141:3, 4, ICB

GOD be in my head
And in my understanding.
God be in my eyes
And in my looking.
God be in my mouth
And in my speaking.
God be in my heart
And in my thinking.

FOR food to eat and those who prepare it;
For health to enjoy it and friends to share it;
Thank you, Heavenly Father.
Amen.

BE present at our table, Lord,
Be here and everywhere adored.
These morsels bless, and grant that we
May feast in Paradise with thee.
Amen.

THANK you for my clothes
And for the food I eat.
Thank you for my house
And the bed in which I sleep.

For friends and grass and trees,
We thank you, Lord above.
For smiling flowers and earth,
And sunny skies above.
We know your tender love.
We thank you for your care,
For light, and fields, and flowers,
And all things everywhere. Amen.

ALL things bright and beautiful,
All creatures, great and small,
All things wise and wonderful,
The Lord God made them all.

Each little flower that opens,
Each little bird that sings,
He made their glowing colors,
He made their tiny wings.

The tall trees in the greenwood,
The meadows where we play,
The rushes by the water
We gather every day—

He gave us eyes to see them,
And lips that we might tell
How great is God Almighty,
Who has made all things well!

Cecil Frances Alexander

LORD of the loving heart,
May mine be loving, too.
Lord of the gentle hands,
May mine be gentle, too.
Lord of the willing feet,
May mine be willing, too.
So may I grow more like to you
In all I say and do. Amen.

Church Missionary Society

DEAR God, you are wise and loving,
You are great and strong;
Glad when we do right,
Grieved when we do wrong.
Father God, my Father,
Guide me every hour;
Keep me safe and shield me
From temptation's power.
Amen.

I will praise you, Lord, with all my heart.
I will tell all the miracles you have done.
I will be happy because of you.
God Most High, I will sing praises to your name.

Psalm 9:1,2, ICB

PRAISE God, from whom all blessings flow;
Praise Him, all creatures here below;
Praise Him above, ye heavenly host;
Praise Father, Son, and Holy Ghost.
Amen.

I hear no voice, I feel no touch,
I see no glory bright;
But yet I know that God is near,
In darkness as in light.

He watches ever by my side,
And hears my whispered prayer:
The Father for his little child
Both night and day doth care.

Now I lay me
down to sleep,
I pray thee, Lord,
thy child to keep:
Thy love guard me
through the night,
And wake me with
the morning light.

I see the moon,
And the moon sees me.
God bless the moon,
And God bless me.